A KIND OF MAGIC

A TRIBUTE TO FREDDIE MERCURY

BY
ROSS
CLARKE

A PERCENTAGE OF THE PROFITS FROM
THIS BOOK WILL BE DONATED TO
THE TERENCE HIGGINS TRUST

1ST PRINTED 1991 • 2ND REPRINT 1991 • REVISED EDITION 1992

THE POWER HOUSE, TANDRIDGE COURT FARM, TANDRIDGE LANE, OXTED, SURREY. RH8 9NJ
PRINTED IN ENGLAND

A little after 7.00pm on Sunday November 24th, 1991, Freddie Mercury, the ultimate showman of pop, died at his home in Kensington, London. His death, at the age of 45, came the day after he admitted that he was suffering from Aids, following months of speculation in the press about his worsening health.

Mercury issued an unexpected statement on Saturday, 23rd November, about his illness, saying he wanted to put the record straight as he knew he had very little time left. He said: "Following the enormous conjuncture in the press, I wish to confirm that I have been tested HIV positive and have Aids.

"I felt it correct to keep this information private to date in order to protect the privacy of those around me. However, the time has now come for my friends and fans around the world to know the truth and I hope that everyone will join with me, my doctors and all those worldwide in the fight against this terrible disease."

A TRAGIC AND LONELY END FOR THE OUTRAGEOUS, FLAMBOYANT AND HIGHLY INNOVATIVE SUPERSTAR WHO CONSTANTLY FLAUNTED HIS BISEXUALITY. HE LOVED HIS WILD LIFESTYLE, ENJOYED RIOTOUS PARTIES AND SPENDING HIS IMMENSE WEALTH - LAVISHING EXPENSIVE GIFTS ON FRIENDS AND LOVERS ALIKE. IT IS ALSO A TRAGEDY THAT THE MAN WHO HAD AN ALMOST UNIQUE TALENT FOR CAPTURING THE EMOTIONS OF AN AUDIENCE SHOULD HAVE DIED A VIRTUAL RECLUSE, WITH THE WORLD DISCUSSING NOT HIS TALENT BUT THE MANNER OF HIS DEATH.

THE CIRCUMSTANCES SURROUNDING HIS DEATH WERE A PARADOX OF THE WAY IN WHICH HE LIVED, AND LOVED, HIS LIFE.

IT IS TO HIS LOVE OF LIFE AND TO HIS MUSIC THAT THIS BOOK IS RESPECTFULLY DEDICATED.

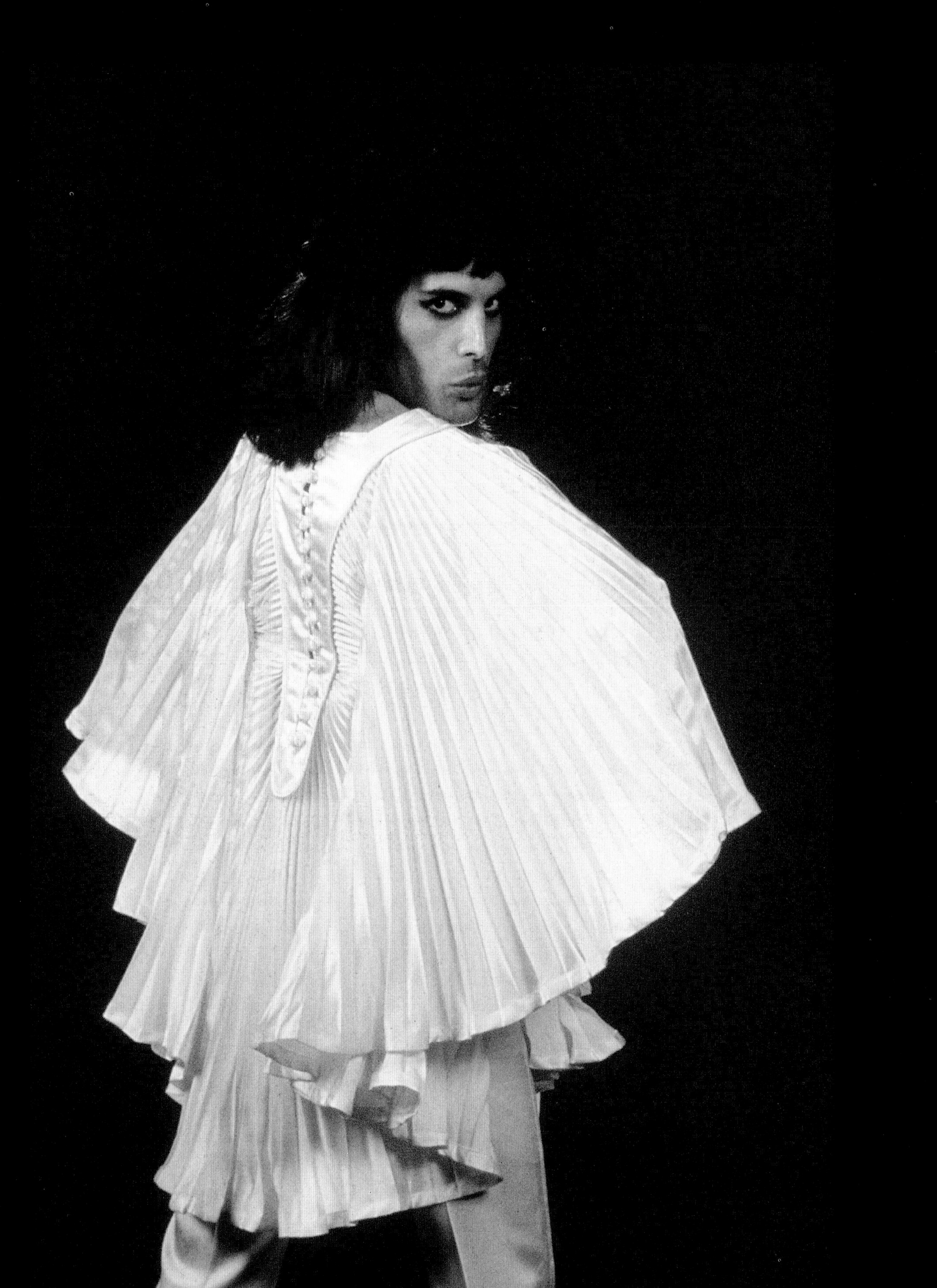

Freddie Mercury

1946 - 1991

A Tribute

Freddie Mercury was born Frederick Bulsara on September 5th, 1946 in Zanzibar. His father, Bomi Bulsara, was a British Government accountant of Persian descent. Freddie and his sister Kashmira, spent their early childhood in luxury in the family mansion in Bombay India, during the last days of the Raj. As he grew older, the youngster attended St Peter's boarding school in Bombay. These were halcyon days. The diplomatic family were wealthy and were treated like royalty by their servants. However, their privileged existence vanished when Bomi was transferred to England and the family were forced to live in a semi-detached house close to Heathrow Airport in Feltham, Middlesex.

Arriving for the first time in England at the age of 14 was a nightmare for Freddie. He was an outsider from the beginning, teased mercilessly by other children because of his colonial accent and foreign looks. This disruption had no real detrimental effect on his education and he left school with three 'O' Levels in Art History and Geography and an 'A' Level in Art. The experience did leave Freddie however, determined to use the fact that he was different to his financial advantage so he would never again have to suffer the indignity of having to endure an ordinary existence.

The quickest way to achieve this, he decided was to become a rock star and defying his conservative family's express wishes he enrolled at Ealing College of Art in West London, a breeding ground turning out rock stars such as The Who's Pete Townsend and Ron Wood of the Stones. Freddie proceeded to study graphic art and made his singing debut with college band

Wreckage. He also began to develop his songwriting techniques and stage persona. He re-christened himself Mercury after the Greek gods' mythological messenger and during the next twenty years his messages would be conveyed to millions of fans.

While Freddie was graduating from Ealing College with a Diploma in Art and Design, three students studying at London's Imperial college were building up a steady following on the London pub and college circuits in a band called Smile.

Some three years earlier, guitarist Brian May had advertised on the college noticeboard inviting other student/musicians to join him in forming a band with which to combine their studies. The first to accept the offer was bassist/vocalist Tim Staffell, followed by drummer Roger Taylor. Despite their studies, the three members of Smile were serious about a long-term career and signed a recording contract to American label, Mercury, who put them in the studio with producer John Anthony. The result was a Tim Staffell song entitled 'Earth', backed with 'Step On Me', a May/Staffell collaboration. The single was released in the US and was an unmitigated disaster.

In the summer of 1970, Tim Staffell quit Smile to sing in ex-Bee Gee Colin Peterson's new band, Humpy Bong, leaving May and Taylor somewhat depressed. May had by this time acquired an honours degree in Physics and was undertaking postgraduate studies in the field of Infra-red Astronomy and Taylor had procured a straightforward degree in Biology. Both were uncertain of their future, consequently, May took a temporary job teaching mathematics whilst pondering his future, and Taylor ran a second-hand clothes stall in Kensington Market.

Taylor was helped in the market by Staffell's flatmate - also a vocalist - who had very definite ideas on how to present a rock band. A tall, handsome young man who painted his nails black and wore feather boas. His name was Freddie Mercury and he was invited to join the line-up - promptly transforming it under the double entendre banner of Queen. They worked with a succession of bass players until science graduate John Deacon was recruited in February 1971.

Freddie, commenting on his choice of Queen as the band's monicker, said: "Years ago I thought up the name Queen...It's just a name, but it's very regal obviously, and it sounds splendid. It's a strong name, very universal and immediate. It had a lot of visual potential and was open to all sorts of interpretations. I was certainly aware of the gay connotations, but that was just one facet of it."

For the remainder of 1971, the four musicians rehearsed, wrote songs and played at friends' parties and small gigs around the West Country. They also played their unique blend of R&B, rock 'n' roll and original material at the Imperial College more than once or twice, but Brian May was reluctant to commit the band to another recording contract after the problems they had encountered whilst being singed to the Mercury label. So it was that Queen remained a part-time outfit. Whilst May studied for his doctorate, Mercury and

Taylor ran their Kensington stall - which now sold artwork as well as clothes - and Deacon taught at a comprehensive school.

Most of their conversations, at this time, revolved around turning professional. All four were eager to take the plunge but were not prepared to sacrifice potentially good careers to have to settle for being second best - they had too much to lose. Then, in 1972, they had their first stroke of real luck.

London-based De Lane Lea studios were looking for a band who would be prepared to show-case their new recording hardware and give demonstrations for potential clients in return for unlimited studio time. Queen were offered the job through a mutual friend and it was this opportunity which was to change the course of their lives.

They took full advantage of the unlimited studio time offered by De Lane Lea and spent most of early 1972 experimenting with the state-of-the-art recording equipment. They recorded various demos including 'Liar', and 'The Night Comes Down' at De Lane Lea.

Many studio technicians came to view the De Lane Lea/Queen show-cases, including Roy Thomas Baker and John Anthony from neighbouring Trident Studios in Wardour Street. They were so impressed by the band that they approached their employers, Barry and Norman Sheffield, and suggested that they sign them to their newly formed production company - Trident Audio Productions.

Despite being impressed by the demos that Queen had produced, the Sheffield brothers wanted to see the band perform live and, after attending a gig at The Pheasantry, a club in the Kings Road, the Trident executives signed them to a production, publishing and management deal.

Dave Thomas, an employee of Trident said later: "When the band walked into the room you just knew they were a class act. They were just a bunch of students but they exuded this amazing charismatic energy - particularly Freddie. He was totally larger than life, quite awe-inspiring."

Producers Baker and Anthony immediately took them into Trident and the recording of their debut album commenced. Concurrently, Trident employed American A&R man, Jack Nelson, to secure the band a recording contract with a major record company. Armed with a 24-track demo and many of Freddie's rather off-the-wall ideas for the presentation of the band, Nelson did not find this a particularly easy task. Eventually, however, he finally found them a home with British giants, EMI, who intended to use the debut album as a launch-pad for a new heavy rock label.

April 1973 saw the EMI promotion machine grind into action, launching Queen at a gig at London's Marquee. The music press attended, EMI record company executives attended, punters attended. Queen performed a soaring, exuberant gig - promoting their debut album entitled 'Queen' for all their worth. Unfortunately

AS IS OFTEN THE WAY IN THE MUSIC BUSINESS, EMI WERE TO TAKE A FURTHER THREE MONTHS TO PLACE THE ALBUM IN THE SHOPS - THUS LOSING THE IMPETUS OF THE CAMPAIGN.

FURTHERMORE, WHEN EMI FINALLY DID RELEASE THE ALBUM, THEY DID SO WITH SUCH PROMOTIONAL RAZZMATAZZ THAT THEY WERE ACCUSED OF 'HYPING' THE BAND AND PERHAPS, AS A CONSEQUENCE, THE FIRST SINGLE 'KEEP YOURSELF ALIVE' RECEIVED VIRTUALLY NO AIR-PLAY. HOWEVER, THE ALBUM EARNED PARTICULAR PRAISE FOR FREDDIE'S UNIQUE VOCAL POWER AND THE TALENTED GUITAR WORK OF BRIAN MAY, ALL PLAYED ON HIS FAMOUS HAND-BUILT GUITAR MADE FROM THE WOOD OF A HUNDRED YEAR-OLD

Mott The Hoople booked the band to support them again in America the following year. Booking agency MAM immediately signed them up for a headline tour of the UK to take place in the spring of 1974, to coincide with the release of their second album.

The music press, however, had their own views on the band who fashioned a unique combination of heavy metal thunder, complex vocal harmonies and a preposterous glamrock image. In short, they were unimpressed.

Fortunately, Queen found unlikely champions in the BBC2 TV programme 'The Old Grey Whistle Test', who played 'Keep Yourself Alive' to the accompaniment of a film clip. This gave them some much needed public exposure leading to Radio One recording one of their live sets. So then, when their second single 'Seven Seas Of Rhye' was released in early 1974, it picked up heavy air-play on Radio One, a medium which had previously eluded them, which translated into sales and reached No. 10 in the charts

A slot on BBC1 TV's 'Top Of The Pops' followed and a UK tour. As the band began to grow in confidence, so showman Freddie's stage performance became more outrageous. He was determined that Queen was going to make it to the top - and stay there. At a show in Scotland, Freddie got the audience so excited that they rioted after the band refused to come back for a fourth encore! At another show, he got too close to his fans, who dragged him off stage. It was this reception that finally bought Queen press recognition.

On this high, the band left for America where they were to support Mott The Hoople again. Halfway through the tour, Brian May fell seriously ill suffering from a stomach ulcer. They were forced to return to Britain and began making their third album without him.

However the enforced lay-off proved to be a turning point in their career, and they bounced back in October 1974 with a new single 'Killer Queen' which took the charts by storm. It was followed by 'Sheer Heart Attack', their best album to that date. With

both releases high in the charts, the band set out on British and European tours. Opening the shows was a dynamic 'Now I'm Here', with dry ice streaming onto the stage - first indication of the special effects and large lighting rig which were to become their trademarks.

The band also took to wearing elaborate costumes - instigated by Freddie - like silk capes, designed by Zandra Rhodes. These costumes, he was to explain later, compensated for the insecurity he felt when on stage. It was this insecurity in himself which was probably responsible for much of the dramatic excess in which he would later indulge.

'Sheer Heart Attack' topped the UK charts, made the TOP TEN in both America and Japan, and the ensuing touring took them across the world with phenomenal success. Freddie fell in love with Japan during Queen's first trip there to promote the album and became a fanatical collector of Japanese art and antiquities. During their tour of Japan, Queen-mania reigned and the band were mobbed at every step by

They returned to Britain to work on their fourth album and most ambitious project to date. They rehearsed the material for two months but, despite this, the recording sessions became more and more complex. The album was 'A Night At The Opera' and the band were determined that it would be something special, something unique and original - an impudent melting together of grand opera and heavy metal. They wanted to achieve this without the use of synthesizers and at least six different recording studios were used - often with one band member playing in a different studio to the rest of the group! Painstakingly, Roy Thomas Baker pieced the whole project together.

In the middle of this, they split acrimoniously with Trident, their production-management company, and took on Elton John's clever but quick-tempered manager, John Reid, to handle their business affairs.

Freddie venomously commented: "As far as Queen are concerned our old management is deceased. They cease to exist in any capacity with us whatsoever. One leaves them behind like one leaves excreta. We feel so relieved!" Trident promptly responded by dumping all their musical equipment into an alley, adjacent to the studio, in the pouring rain!

In October 1975, EMI released the six-minute classical pastiche, 'Bohemian Rhapsody' as a single. Initially, EMI were reluctant to put out the track, fearing it was too long. However, it was disc jockey Kenny Everett who helped make up their minds and those of the band, by declaring it a smash hit.

Kenny Everett had become a close friend and confident of Freddy and, in an interview with London's Capital Radio, he recalled: "I got a call in 1975 from Freddy who said 'Ken, I was in the studios the other day and I've finished off this new single. But it's about eight minutes long and I don't know whether it's going to be a hit'.

"I said, 'Bring it over, we'll stick it on

one of my tape machines in the studio and give it a listen. I doubt if anyone will play it if it's as long as that because people are frightened of long records'. So Freddy brought it over and plonked it on the machine and, of course, this glorious operatic wonder of 'Bohemian Rhapsody came out. I said, Oh forget about it, it could be half an hour long it's going to be No. 1 for centuries.'

"He was very unsure about this piece of genius. It was very odd when you look back on it in retrospect, because it was so great. It's like Mozart saying: 'I don't know whether my clarinet concerto is going to take off'. It's silly really. I mean it's got No.1 written all over it from the first note."

'Bohemian Rhapsody' went straight to No. 1 and stayed there for nine weeks. The 1975 UK tour began before the album 'A Night At The Opera' was released but, by the time the tour ended, the album was also securely placed at the top of the chart. Such was Queen's popularity at the start of 1976 that all four albums released to that date appeared simultaneously in the top 30.

This single also marked the beginning of the video revolution in pop music. 'Bohemian Rhapsody' was accompanied by an artfully directed video which at the time became essential viewing on BBC1's 'Top Of The Pops'. It led to the pop video becoming a prerequisite for a song in the charts and often receiving more skill and imagination than the song it accompanies.

The single marked a strange but clear departure from the heavy rock that had dominated the earlier Queen albums. It was always apparent that there were two sides to Queen, and suddenly the other one had taken over. Perhaps it was an experiment but the wisdom to their stylistic change was reflected in the enormous success of 'Bohemian Rhapsody'. It was granted an award by the British Phonographic Industry as the best record of the last twenty-five years. This single undeniably ensured that Queen became one of the biggest bands in the world. Things couldn't have been better.

The tour which coincided with this phenomenal success, saw the band playing longer sets than ever before. They became ever more spectacular events in keeping with the grandiose splendour of their music, employing vast sets and lighting rigs. An entire show was filmed by the BBC, who broadcast the Christmas Eve gig at the Hammersmith Odeon on BBC2, and live in stereo on Radio One.

Freddie set out to stage a huge camp-rock cabaret for a breathless world audience desperate for glamour. Deacon and May were both naturally retiring types and Taylor was stuck behind his drums, so the band relied heavily on Freddie's commanding stage presence. His flamboyant costumes ranged from full drag to sequinned, skin- tight jump-suits. He preened his way through a myriad of costume changes, singing in his unique, majestic voice which could scale operatic heights and leave his audiences begging for mercy as he tried to bully them into joining his impossible scales. He always matched up to the demands of projecting Queen's music and image to the four corners of the world's biggest stadiums.

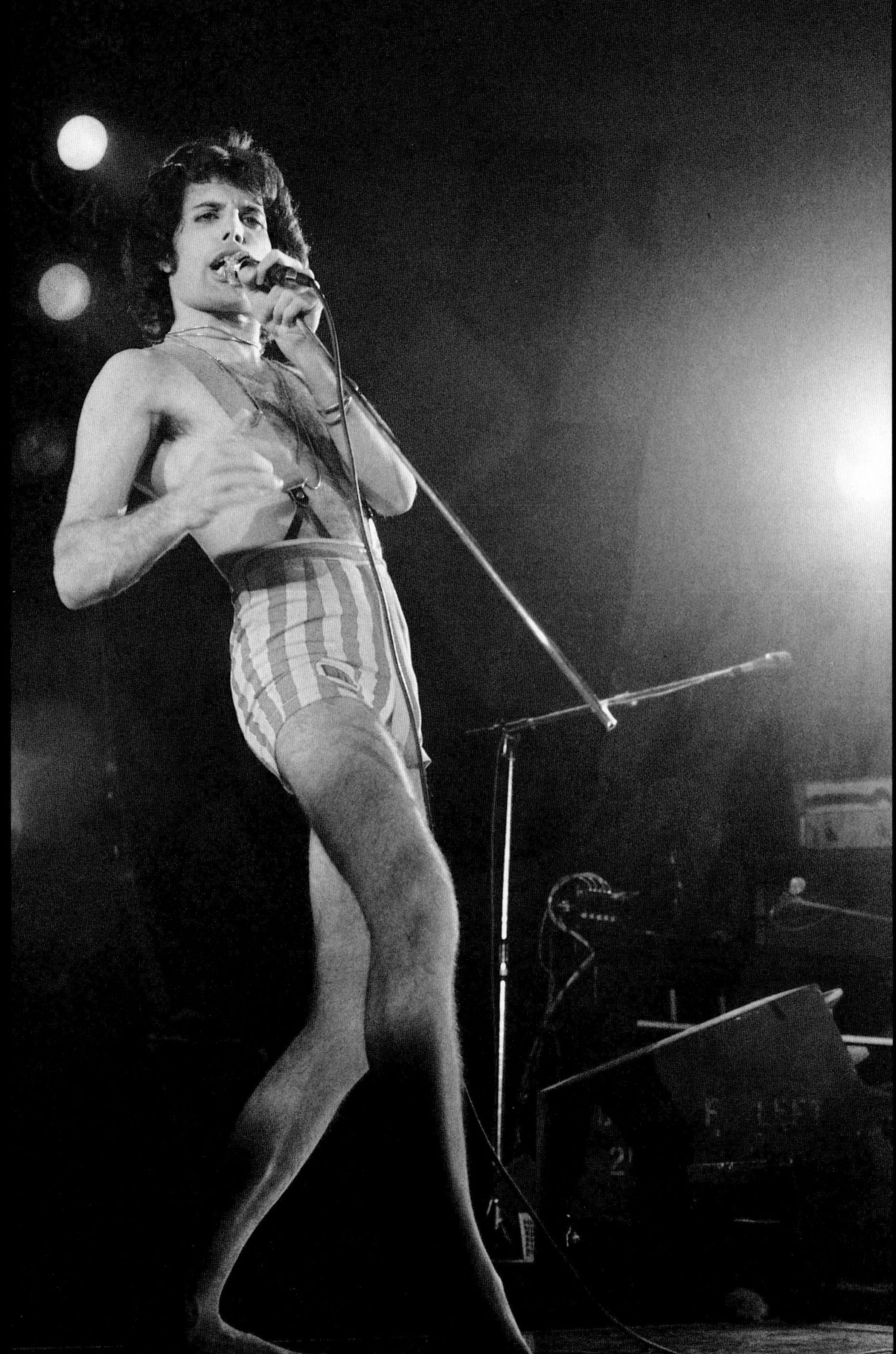

Freddie's panache and style offered fans thrills and fantasies and won him the kind of adoration usually reserved for Hollywood idols.

A second single from the album was released in the summer of 1976 - 'You're My Best Friend' followed by a notable free concert in London's Hyde Park in September. Over 150,000 fans turned up, one of Britain's best-attended shows ever.

Brian May has fond memories of the gig. 'The Hyde Park concert was really high. The occasion rather than the gig. You know, the tradition of Hyde Park. I went to see the first one with Pink Floyd and Jethro Tull - a great atmosphere and the feeling that it was free. We felt that it would be nice to try and revive that but it was fraught with heartache because there were so many problems. Trying to get the place was hard enough, let alone the evening. We had to make compromises and in the end, because the schedule overran by half an hour, we couldn't do an encore."

The event was not only filmed, but also broadcast on Capital Radio. It gained the band enormous respect in the music business and re-confirmed their entry into rock's first division.

By this time the money was starting to pour in, along with an Ivor Novello songwriting award for 'Bohemian Rhapsody' and Freddie settled into his favourite role 24 hours a day - living the rock 'n' roll dream, high on excess.

Freddie's love of the bizarre and dramatic on a huge scale was not confined to the stage. His private life was just as over the top. He paid £500,000 for his Edwardian mansion, 'Garden Lodge' at 1 Logan Place in Kensington, West London which boasted high walls and a secret garden. Within months he was turning down £4 million for the sanctuary. There was the Manhattan apartment to decorate and he bought antiques enough to stock a museum.

Then there was the drinking - Freddie could allegedly down a bottle of vodka. His

favourite tipple, in one sitting - and the infamous never-ending parties.

Guests at one of his birthday parties were sent first-class tickets to fly to New York aboard Concorde for the bash. The party went on for days and Freddie spent more than £50,000 on champagne alone. For one after-show party he hired a body-painter from Germany and guests were surprised to find the 'uniformed' bell boys parading amongst them serving drinks and food were, in fact, naked. At a banquet in New Orleans he hid a nude model in a huge tray of raw liver. It wasn't long before Freddie's name was a byword of excess and decadence. It was also associated with an extraordinary generosity.

Freddie never made a secret of his bisexuality saying: "I've had a lot of lovers. I've tried relationships on either side - male and female. But all of them went wrong." He also commented: "Love is Russian roulette for me. I try to hold back when I'm attracted to someone but I just can't control love. It runs riot. All my one night

stands are just me playing a part." Real friends suspected that his promiscuity sprang from loneliness. Freddie, prince of attitude-strikers, needed a constant audience and his nightmare was walking into an empty bedroom.

However, there was one important woman in his life, reportedly the only person he ever truly loved, blonde Mary Austin. The two met in 1970 when Mary was a shop manageress in Biba boutique and Freddie was just another aspiring singer. They lived together for seven years, an arrangement which fell victim to his growing fame and bisexuality.

"I would have married him if he had been a heterosexual," Mary has said. "I was devastated when we stopped living together, but strangely enough, our closeness just grew over the years."

When the couple split up, Freddie - generous as ever - bought her a £400,000 four-bedroom house in Kensington, a stones' throw from his own home. Two years later,

When the romance was rekindled, she asked Freddie to give her a child - an invitation which he declined stating "I'd rather have another cat." More recently he gave his blessing to Mary having a child by becoming godfather to her first son Richard.

The sequel to 'A Night At The Opera' was the album 'A Day At The Races', released on 12th December 1976. It was preceded by a single 'Someone To Love' which went to No.2 in the UK charts. 'A Day At The Races' was launched with over half a million advance orders in the UK alone, and reached No.1 for Christmas.

1977 began with a two-month tour of America, supported by rock band Thin Lizzy. The US critics slammed Queen whilst raving about Lizzy. Instead of this being defamatory to Queen, they won an army of new fans who attended the gigs to check out Thin Lizzy on the critics' recommendations!

real Queen's Silver Jubilee. The band returned to England and finished off their British tour with two nights at London's Earls Court as part of the official Jubilee celebrations, putting on a lavish show and losing £75,000 in the process, so costly were the lighting and other effects. These gigs were Queen at their grandest, with Freddie's vocals showing a breathtaking range and ability to switch styles from ballads to frenetic rock numbers. Roger Taylor's drumming and backing vocals were equally effective, and Brian May's guitar work was simply quite amazing.

However, they received savage reviews in the music press, who reflected the general climate of antagonism towards bands who portrayed any kind of glamour. To them, Freddie Mercury - who toasted his audience with champagne - was the personification of all that was wrong with rock. The New Musical Express ran a feature which can only be described as a confrontation between Freddie and journalist Tony Stewart under the heading 'Is This Man A Prat?'

Taylor recalled a wonderful moment when Freddie and Sid Vicious met face to face. "We were recording an album next door to The Sex Pistols. One day Sid Vicious stumbled in and yelled at Freddie 'Ullo Fred, so you've really bought ballet to the masses then?' Freddie just turned round and said 'Ah, Mr. Ferocious. Well, we're trying our best dear!'"

Queen retreated to the recording studios to make yet another album, although they had only a three-month break before the next US tour was due to begin. The album, 'News Of The World', was to prove to be a turning point in both style and content with the lavish production and full harmonies of earlier releases replaced by the highly innovative Freddie with an altogether harsher sound. It was with this album that they finally cracked America wide open, with the single 'We Are The Champions' achieving Platinum status and becoming an anthem at their shows. The song went on to become a standard sing-along chorus at sporting events of every kind and was even adopted by the Labour Party during their 1991 Party conference!

It was during this period that Freddie spoke of his ability to keep breaking new ground, in his own inimitable style: "I just like to think that we've come through rock 'n' roll, call it what you like, and there are no barriers. It's open. Especially now when everybody's putting their feelers out and they want to infiltrate new territories. This is what I've been trying to do for years. Nobody's incorporated ballet. I mean, it sounds so outrageous and so extreme but I know there's going to come a time when it's commonplace.

"The term rock 'n' roll is just a label one starts off with. I should like to think of it as a vast open door. We just carry on doing as many things as we can in different fields. Labels are confusing, they bounce off me. People want art. They want showbiz. They want to see you rush off in your limousine. We will stick to our guns, and if we're worth anything we will live on."

After a lengthy American tour, a month in Europe and four UK dates, including two nights at Wembley's Empire Pool, Queen went to Europe to record a new album, once again recruiting the aid of Roy Thomas Baker as producer. These sessions produced the strangest album to that date, 'Jazz', which emerged with a distinctive American feel. It was two tracks from this album which were responsible for the most outrageous publicity campaign ever seen.

Brian May had a track called 'Fat Bottomed Girls' and Freddie had one called 'Bicycle Race'. It was decided, therefore, to stage a bicycle race between several dozen nude girls which was filmed by Steve Wood at Wimbledon Stadium. The event was meant simply as 'a bit of fun' but it left the band wide open to charges of sexploitation by the ever vigilant music press. Old enemy The New Musical Express even ran a suitable picture of Freddie with the caption 'Fat Bottomed Queen'.

The band were determined not to bow to pressure by the press and, during the subsequent tour of America, brought

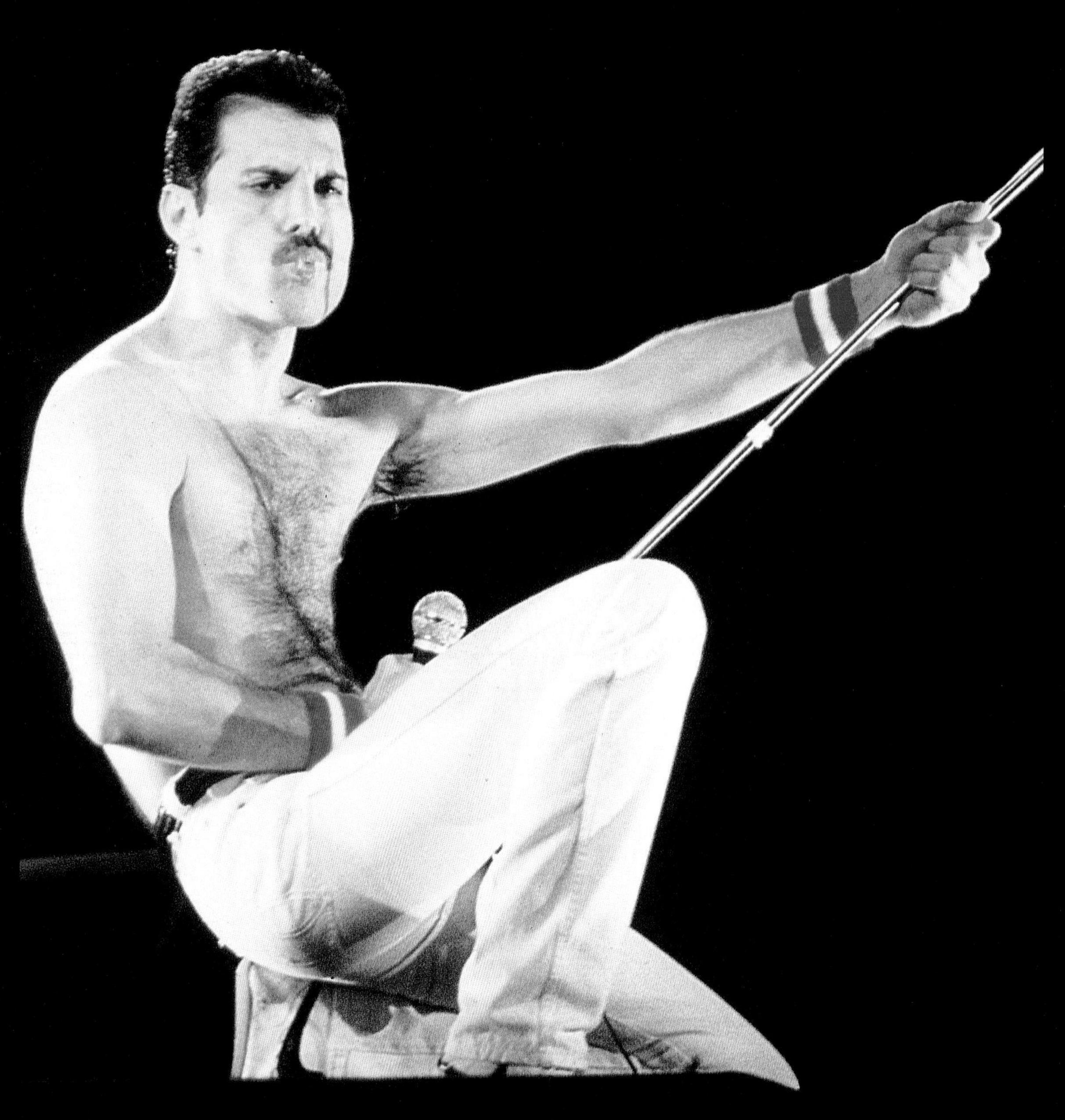

UEEN

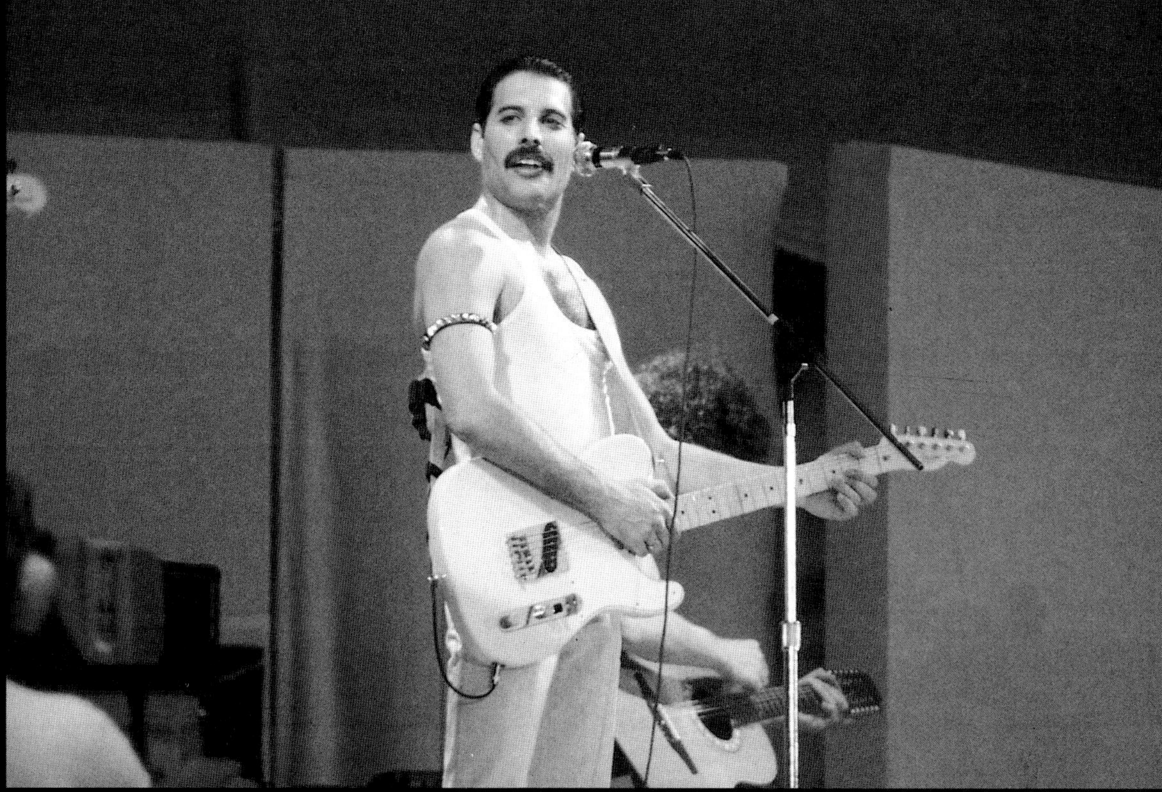

girls on stage during the 'Jazz' section. This did absolutely nothing to quieten the controversy. However, not surprisingly, American fans flocked to see the shows, and the gigs at New York's prestigious Madison Square Garden were completely sold out.

A two month European tour at the start of 1979 led into a month's stay in Japan and the European dates were recorded. A double album, 'Live Killers' was released during the summer to a complete panning from critics and from Roger Taylor, who hated the album and said so publicly. The main criticism was due to the inclusion of 'Bohemian Rhapsody', during which Queen left the stage while the audience were subjected to pre-recorded tapes.

Brian May said at the time: "'Bohemian Rhapsody' isn't a stage number. People don't like us leaving the stage but, to be honest, I'd rather leave than play to a backing track. It's a totally false situation. We would rather be up-front about it because it's not something that can be played onstage. It was multi-layered in the studio but we play it at gigs because people want to hear it."

The album was, in many ways a disappointment. The overall balance of the album was weighted towards the later albums and there was nothing at all from 'Queen II' and only one song from the debut album. It included several mistakes, for reasons best known to the band, and several of the tracks were very poorly mixed.

The release of 'Live Killers', however, allowed them to take their time over their next studio offering. In taking their time, they created hits like 'Crazy Little Thing Called Love' and 'Save Me'.

During this period, John Reid was relieved of his duties as their business manager and the band opted to manage themselves. Bass player, John Deacon, the least conspicuous member of Queen developed a flair for the business side of their activities and took full control.

Also in the summer, Freddie finally got a chance to take part in some ballet, when Derek Dean and Wayne Eagling invited him to join them onstage at the Royal Ballet. They had devised a dance interpretation of 'Bohemian Rhapsody' and 'Killer Queen'. Freddie rehearsed for months. Needless to say, the music press totally ignored the event.

November 1979 saw Queen return to tour Britain with the single 'Crazy Little Thing Called Love' climbing the charts. The 'Crazy Tour' saw the band return to playing small venues which was a nice gesture to their fans. The end result was spectacular, and they varied their set list from night to night. Freddie took the opportunity to diversify, on stage, to macho leather gear and stalked the stage like a panther to the delight of the audience.

Freddie said later: "I wrote 'Crazy Little Thing Called Love' in the bath. I actually dragged an upright piano to my bedside once. I've been known to scribble lyrics in the middle of the night without putting the lights on."

On Boxing Day, they played a special charity show at the Hammersmith Odeon, in aid of the Kampuchea appeal, where their set was filmed and recorded.

The year ended on a high, with Queen announcing that they had been invited to write the sound-track for the Dino de Laurentiis production of 'Flash Gordon'. They accepted the invitation - their first movie sound-track.

By the end of this decade, Queen had sold over 45 million albums worldwide and the band members were amongst Britain's highest paid executives - drawing annual salaries of around £700,000 from their company, Queen Productions Ltd. And that didn't include royalties, which were stacking up even faster than the string of Queen hits!

The band's popularity continued unabated into the Eighties. At the beginning of 1980, they had to contend with the hectic

schedule of recording both the 'Flash Gordon' sound-track and 'The Game' - their new album. 'The Game' was released in June and went straight into the UK album charts at No.1, with the single 'Another One Bites The Dust' (penned by John Deacon) following in July. It entered the UK Top Ten but took the US by storm, becoming No.1 in both the pop and soul chart simultaneously.

John Deacon said: "I listened to a lot of soul music when I was in school and I've always been interested in that sort of music. I'd been wanting to do a track like 'Another One Bites The Dust' for a while. I could hear it as a song for dancing but had no idea it would become as big as it did. The song got picked up off our album and some of the black radio stations in the US started playing it, which we've never had before."

The sound-track for 'Flash Gordon' was a very exciting project for the band. It was the first time a rock group had complete control over the entire score. They were given the finished film to watch and knew that had to do something over the top to

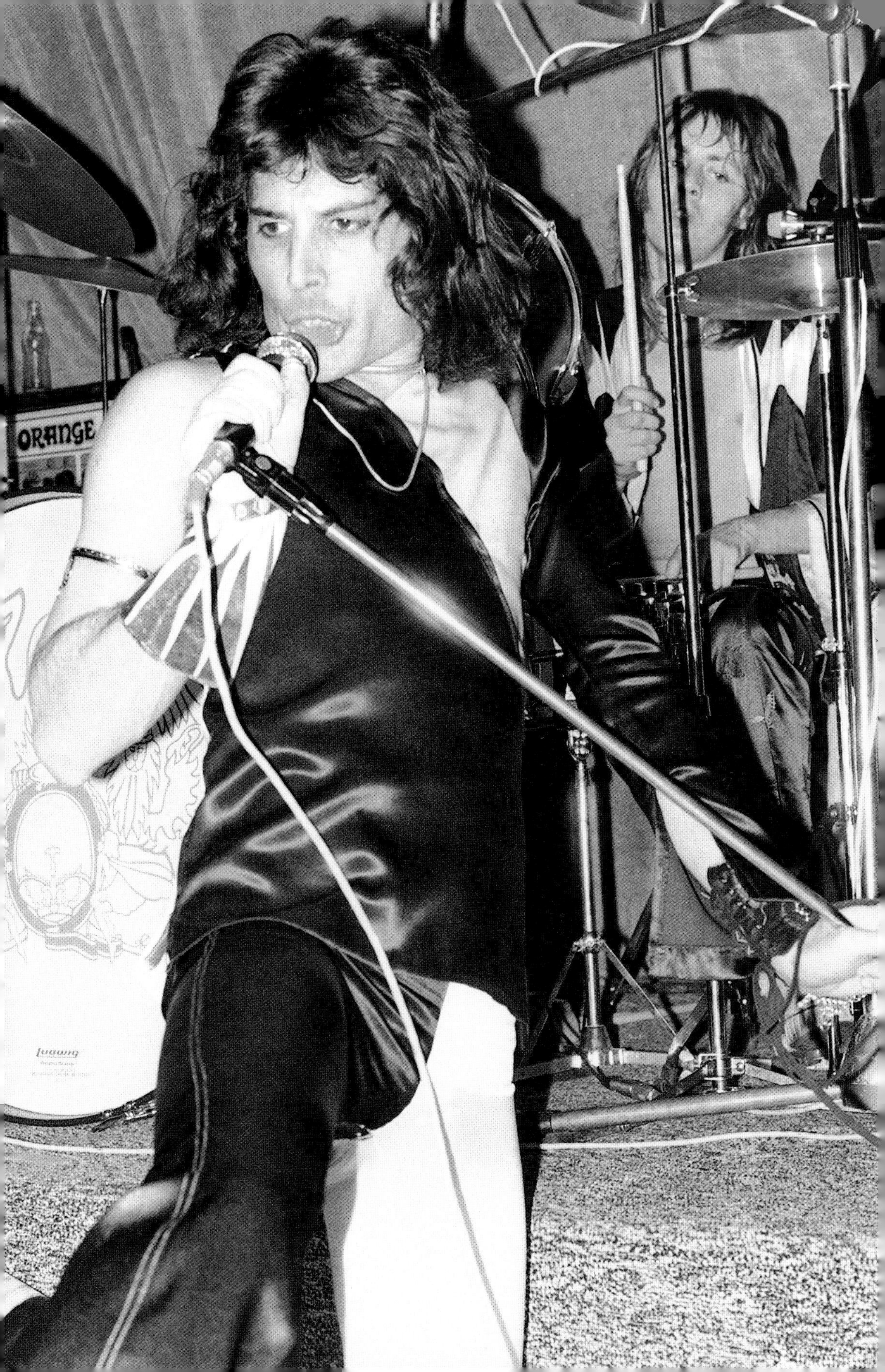
ORANGE
Ludwig

Fender JAZZ BASS

COMPLEMENT THE MOVIE. THE FINISHED SCORE FINALLY EMERGED, BUT NOT UNTIL THEY HAD EXHAUSTED THE TECHNOLOGY OF FOUR DIFFERENT RECORDING STUDIOS!

QUEEN SET ABOUT THE ENDLESS TOURING TO PROMOTE 'THE GAME', STARTING IN AMERICA. BY THE TIME THE TOUR ARRIVED IN EUROPE, THE BAND WERE ABOUT TO RELEASE THEIR 'FLASH GORDON' SOUND-TRACK, AND SO 'FLASH' AND 'THE HERO', TWO TRACKS FROM THE ALBUM, WERE ADDED TO THEIR LIVE SET. THE BRITISH SHOWS DURING DECEMBER FOUND THE BAND IN SPARKLING FORM AND THE SET VARIED EACH NIGHT. ON ONE PARTICULARLY NOTABLE NIGHT, 9TH DECEMBER, THEY PLAYED 'IMAGINE' AS A SPECIAL TRIBUTE TO JOHN LENNON WHO HAD BEEN TRAGICALLY ASSASSINATED THE DAY BEFORE.

FREDDIE, SPEAKING OF HIS AUDIENCE: "I LIKE PEOPLE TO GO AWAY FROM A QUEEN SHOW FEELING FULLY ENTERTAINED, HAVING HAD A GOOD TIME. I THINK QUEEN SONGS ARE PURE ESCAPISM, LIKE GOING TO SEE A GOOD FILM - AFTER THAT, THEY CAN GO AWAY AND SAY THAT WAS GREAT, AND GO BACK TO ALL THEIR PROBLEMS.

'I don't want to change the world with our music. There are no hidden messages in our songs. I like to write songs for fun, for modern consumption. People can discard them like a used tissue afterwards. You listen to it, like it, discard it, then on to the next. Disposable pop."

Brian May reflected on Queen's attitude to performing: "We do have a lot of power. We just hope that we can divert it in the right direction. Our fans are sensible people, they're creating the situation as much as we are, it's not that we're just leading them like sheep. You play the music which excites people, which interests them. It's rock 'n' roll, there's no philosophical reason why we should be there. Touring is the most immediately fulfiling part of what we do, and it's not really a big strain - mentally or physically - because we're well organised and we know how to do it. All you have to worry about is playing well on the night. Suddenly, life becomes simple again."

Following the British dates, Queen relaxed until the next leg took them to Japan in 1981. Freddie spent some of the time at his home in Kensington, something which had so far eluded him due to the constant recording and touring demands. Freddie explained: "Every person who makes a lot of money has a dream he wants to carry out, and I achieved that dream with this wonderful house. Whenever I watched Hollywood movies set in plush homes with lavish decor, I wanted that for myself and now I've got it. But to me it was much more important to get the damn thing than to actually go and live in it. Maybe the challenge has worn off now. I'm very much like that - once I get something I'm not that keen on it anymore. I still love my house, but the real enjoyment is that I've achieved it."

Poignantly, Freddie went on: "Sometimes, when I'm alone at night, I imagine that when I'm about 50 I'll creep into that house as my refuge and then I'll start making it a home." Unhappily, this was to be a prediction which was to come true several years later.

In Japan Freddie was able to indulge in one of his favourite pastimes, splashing out a

fortune in Japanese art and antiques which were to decorate his homes. It was also suggested that he would spend hours on the phone baby-talking to his beloved cats Oscar and Tiffany, in London!

Spring 1981 saw Queen achieve a major first by touring South America. The first of their eight concerts in Brazil and Argentina attracted a total audience of over half a million people and their concert in Sao Paulo was performed before a world-record paying audience of 231,000.

They were the first major rock act to tour this continent and they did so in style although it was a massive task. it went out under the banner 'Gluttons For Punishment Tour'! They flew 20 tons of sound equipment from Japan, a further 40 ton load from Miami (including a full football field covering of artificial turf, to protect the ground in the arenas they were due to play) plus 16 tons of stage scaffolding from Los Angeles. The tour had taken a year to organise and had estimated running costs of £25,000 per day. However, the gamble paid off and the audiences were the most enthusiastic and warm that the band had ever seen. Freddie said: "We were all terribly nervous. We had no right to automatically expect the works from an alien territory. I don't think they'd ever seen such an ambitious show, with all the lighting and effects."

Back in Europe, recording had commenced on the 'Hot Space' album at Queen's Mountain studios in Montreux. These sessions were to lead to a surprise collaboration with David Bowie on 'Under Pressure'. David Bowie explained: "They turned up in Montreux, so I went to see them in the studio and we just started one of those inevitable jams, which led to a skeleton of a song. I thought it was quite a nice tune so we finished it off. It sort of half came off, but I think it could have been a lot better. It was a rush thing, one of those things that took place over twenty four hours. I think it stands up better as a demo. It was done so quickly that some of it makes me cringe a bit, but the idea I like."

The single made No. 1 in the UK charts Queen's first since 'Bohemian Rhapsody' and

No.9 in the US. The album, Hot Space and its first single 'Body Language' provoked controversy because of the apparent shift towards a more disco/funk based sound. However, some stunning shows during that year's tour soon silenced the critics' hasty ill-informed judgement.

To mark their tenth anniversary, Queen released not only their 'Greatest Hits' album, but also 'Greatest Flix', a video compilation, and 'Greatest Pix', a book which reproduced articles about the band by the likes of Paul Gambaccini and Ray Coleman together with lots of interesting photographs. The book was compiled by Jacques Lowe, former official photographer for the White House during the Kennedy era.

The 'Greatest Hits' album was rarely out of the UK chart for the following two years.

During 1982, Queen toured almost constantly taking in Europe, America and Japan. Little wonder, then, that they decided to take 1983 off from recording and touring - their first sabbatical since their inception.

Exhaustion apart, the band were finding that they were getting on each other's nerves. The solution, they decided would be to spend the year following solo pursuits, enabling them to come back together as Queen with a fresh perspective. There actually was talk of the band splitting up, but they felt that perhaps this would have been foolhardy. Brian explained "We didn't want to split up because we felt that's a mistake that many people have made from The Beatles onwards. It would have been so good if they could have held together longer. No matter how talented the individuals are, the group is always something more than it's components. We think Queen is an example of a proper group. With all its shortcomings, we think it's worth keeping together".

"We've experimented a lot in the past and some of the experiments didn't work. Our last album was one big experiment and a lot of people totally hated it - it really didn't sell very well. We've had ups and downs

People don't realise that. They think Queen can't do anything wrong."

Freddie commented: "I used to think we'd go on for five years, but it's got to the point where we are actually too old to break up. Can you imagine forming a new band at 40? Be a bit silly, wouldn't it?"

In 1984, Queen broke their silence by appearing at the San Remo Song Festival. The gig was almost a disaster due to May and Taylor having a horrific fight over the choice of material amongst other things. Fortunately, Freddie saved the day, and possibly the band, with his arch sense of humour, by cracking them both up with laughter.

One of the other acts at the San Remo Song Festival was Culture Club. Freddie was terribly impressed: "Boy George is a great talent. That boy is so brave".

"When I started off, rock bands were all wearing jeans and suddenly here's Freddie Mercury in a Zandra Rhodes frock

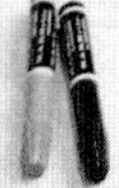

with make-up and black nail varnish. It was totally outrageous. In a way, Boy George has just updated that thing, the whole glam-rock bit. George is more like a drag queen. It's the same outrage, just doubled."

Their new album, 'The Works' was a huge success and spawns four hit singles – 'Radio Ga Ga', 'I Want To Break Free', 'It's A Hard Life' and 'Hammer to Fall'. A full European tour followed into late summer lasting well into 1985. The success of the album and the singles ensured that the dates were quickly sold out.

'The Works' tour then controversially moved to Sun City in South Africa, putting the band on the United Nations cultural blacklist. Many observers felt that this was a completely irresponsible thing to do. Queen paid dearly with a huge fine and the threat of expulsion from the Musicians Union. The tour itself was far from successful with Freddie developing throat trouble and several dates having to be cancelled. The accusations aimed at Queen by the press, who felt they were breaking the boycott for financial or even racist reasons were unfair. Many of the band's songs deal with freedom - 'White Man', 'I Want To Break Free' and 'Is This The World We Created?' - the chief motivation seems to have been the naive belief that change could be brought about through their music.

Brian May tried to explain their decision to play Sun City: "We're totally against apartheid and all it stands for, but I feel we did a lot of bridge building. We actually met musicians of both colours. They all welcomed us with open arms. The only criticism we got was from outside South Africa."

Whilst the band tried to pour oil on troubled waters, Freddie tried his hand at a solo project. He recorded the single, 'Love Kills' and donated it to Giorgio Moroder, for use in the sound-track of the revamped version of Fritz Lang's classic silent film Metropolis. The single hit No.10 in the UK charts.

Queen stopped off in Munich to record 'Thank God It's Christmas', but took to the

QUEEN

world stage again in January 1985, headlining both nights at the massive Rock In Rio festival in Brazil. The festival is an enormous event and the band must have thought that they'd never face a larger audience. They were wrong.

Bob Geldof's Live Aid began with many of Britain's leading rock acts coming together, in December 1984, to record 'Do They Know It's Christmas'. In six months Band Aid's single went on to become the UK's best ever selling single. Bob Geldof's dream of a massive live event, to raise money for the starving in Ethiopia, was initially dismissed as being impossible to achieve. However, in July 1985, the world's leading rock acts took to the stages of Wembley and Philadelphia. This remarkable event was to be seen, live, by over a billion viewers worldwide.

Queen were invited to participate and instantly agreed. To prepare for the event, they rehearsed solidly for three weeks in order to condense their set into just 20 minutes. With no sound-check and on a bare stage, they turned in the most stunning performance of the event which superseded even Woodstock in the public imagination. It was this performance which, undoubtedly, was the pinnacle of their career.

Freddie was at his best. His dark hair cropped short and wearing light blue jeans and white vest, he set Wembley Stadium alight and turned Queen into the ultimate supergroup. Even Elton John admitted later that Freddie had stolen the show with his exceptional ability to capture the crowd.

All in all, 1985 was a good year for Queen. In May, Freddie released his first solo album, 'Mr. Bad Guy' and a single 'I Was Born To Love You' rested at No.11 in the UK charts.

The Live Aid appearance seemed to revitalise the band and they quickly re-entered the studio to record the album 'A Kind Of Magic'.

A single from the album, 'One Vision', was released in November, and was the first time in the band's career that all four

QUEEN

members had collaborated on a single. The video for the song was, for Queen, positively subdued, portraying the band recording in a studio in Munich. Unfortunately, their publicity machine worked against them on this occasion, when an accompanying press release stated that the song was inspired by Live Aid. As usual, their old enemies the music press, accused them of 'cashing in' on the event an accusation which upset them greatly.

Roger Taylor commented: "I was absolutely devastated when I saw that in the press. It was a terrible mistake and we were really annoyed about it. Some public relations person has obviously got hold of the wrong end of the stick."

In 1986, 'One Vision' forgotten, their single and album 'A Kind Of Magic' became best sellers with the album going straight into the UK charts at No.1. A major European tour was announced for the summer again taking in Wembley Stadium. These shows were on a massive scale, the stage set was huge and the music drawn from all stages in their career. Ticket applications for their two Wembley Stadium shows numbered close to half a million and tickets for their Newcastle gig sold out within one hour of going on sale.

"The queue of ticket applicants at Newcastle was longer than the queue for Cup Final tickets when Newcastle United were in the F.A. Cup Final," top promoter Harvey Goldsmith, told assembled press-men at a press conference. "The Manchester show was the fastest selling show ever to be advertised in that city. We were overwhelmed at the demand for Wembley Stadium tickets, but not surprised. However the rush for the Newcastle and Manchester show went beyond our wildest dreams."

Harvey Goldsmith also announced at the same press conference that Queen would end their dates by headlining an open air concert before an audience of 120,000 at Knebworth Park in August.

Queen's new stage show was based around a 160ft stage - requiring holes to be drilled in the concrete foundations of the

arenas and big enough to fill one end of Wembley stadium - a new Clare Brothers P A system and the largest lighting rig ever assembled. The result was proof that, after 15 years, Queen were one of the best live bands in the world. Certainly, very few who saw the shows were disappointed.

Knebworth proved to be the final Queen show. It was not until May 1989 that they returned with the brilliantly stylish 'The Miracle' album which soon became a huge worldwide hit. However, Freddie embarked on a sporadic solo career. He involved himself in the sound-track of Dave Clarke's musical 'Time' and Freddie's rendition of the title theme reached No.24 in the UK chart. He followed this up in July with his first video EP featuring four tracks: 'I Was Born To Love You', 'Made In Heaven', 'Time' and 'Living On My Own'. Having been banned from TV, the last track became an instant collector's item, depicting

Freddie had his greatest solo success with his cover of The Platter's 1956 hit 'The Great Pretender', a typically overwrought performance which he took to No.4 in the charts.

The year ended on a high note, with the release of 'Live Magic', a recording of the eventful 'Magic Tour'. Even without a single release, it sells 400,000 copies by Christmas and reaches No.3.

In 1987, Freddie teamed up with Spanish opera singer Montserrat Caballe. This unlikely duo recorded a single, 'Barcelona', a mock-operatic folly composed by Freddie which was then mooted as the official anthem of the 1992 Olympics. It is still in contention for that accolade. Freddie explained: "I happened to mention it on Spanish TV and she called me up."

This collaboration culminated in a gala concert, 'La Nit' (The Night) in Barcelona's Avinguda De Maria Cristina. A

TUXEDO-CLAD FREDDIE AND BEFROCKED MS CABALLE PERFORMED 'BARCELONA' WITH A FINALE OF FIREWORKS. THE WORLD'S PRESS WERE GRANTED NO INTERVIEWS.

TO MARK THE OCCASION OF HIS 41ST BIRTHDAY IN 1987, FREDDIE HIRED A DC9 AND FLEW 80 OF HIS FRIENDS TO IBIZA. THERE HE TOOK OVER PIKES, ONE OF THE ISLAND'S MOST EXCLUSIVE HOTELS, AND THREW AN OUTRAGEOUSLY LAVISH PARTY COMPLETE WITH FLAMENCO DANCERS, A FIREWORKS DISPLAY FLASHING HIS NAME IN LIGHTS ACROSS THE SKY AND A 20-FOOT LONG BIRTHDAY CAKE CARRIED BY SIX SPANIARDS, DRESSED IN WHITE AND GOLD.

THE AFFAIR WAS TYPICAL OF THE LIFE HE LIVED - TO THE HILT, IN AN UNASHAMEDLY EXTROVERT, OVER-THE-TOP FASHION. BLESSED WITH WEALTH, LOOKS, TALENT AND PUBLIC ACCEPTANCE OF HIS FOIBLES, FREDDIE HAD EVERY REASON TO THINK HIM SELF IMMORTAL - UNTIL AIDS BEGAN TO STRIKE AT THOSE CLOSEST TO HIM. SUDDENLY, FREDDIE'S JOKEY ARCHNESS AND DEVIL-MAY-CARE ATTITUDE WERE NOT ENOUGH TO BANISH REALITY.

Freddie's renowned bisexual proclivities made him the target of sustained speculation when the Aids epidemic began to take its toll and rumours abounded that he had tested HIV positive.

"Anyone who has been promiscuous should have a test", he said in an interview four years ago. "I'm fine, I'm clear. Previously, I had just lived for sex. Amazingly, I've just gone the other way. Aids just changed my life. I have stopped going out, I've almost become a nun. I was extremely promiscuous but I've stopped all that. What's more, I don't miss that kind of life."

Freddie retreated to his beloved home in Kensington. The house he didn't believe would become a home until he needed sanctuary.

He concentrated on staying alive - his most pressing concern. He refused to be seen in public, preferring instead to spend time in his secluded gardens.

In February 1990, after Queen pulled out at the last minute from an appearance at the BRITS Awards, photographs of a haggard and wan Freddie were circulated. However, in the autumn he was back in the studio with Queen, recording what was to be the band's last album. Entitled 'Innuendo', it entered the UK chart at No.1 in early 1991 and was followed by a compilation 'Greatest Hits II', which also topped the UK charts.

One of his final, reluctant returns to the outside world came in February 1991, when he spent a day with Queen in a TV studio in Wembley recording a £200,000 video to promote the single 'I'm Going Slightly Mad'. He took on the role of the poet, Byron, covering his sunken features with white make-up. Although he smiled dutifully he wore a haunted expression and witnesses were shocked by his dramatic weight loss which had left him gaunt and painfully thin. In spite of these reports, Freddie's spokesman insisted: "He's fine. He enjoyed making the video and he's delighted to be back."

HOWEVER, REPORTS THAT HE WAS VISITED BY DR. BRIAN GIZZARD, HEAD OF THE AIDS UNIT AT LONDON'S WESTMINSTER HOSPITAL, IN EARLY NOVEMBER, ADDED FUEL TO THE RUMOURS THAT FREDDIE WAS CLOSE TO DEATH

FOR MANY, THE DEATH OF FREDDIE MERCURY IS THE DEATH OF AN ERA BUT, THROUGH HIS MUSIC, HIS ENORMOUS TALENT, ENDURING PERSONALITY AND ARCH SENSE OF HUMOUR HE WILL CONTINUE TO LIVE ON FOR EVER.

FAREWELL TO FREDDIE

The news of Freddie Mercury's death shocked the world. Friends and fans paid tribute to the genius and kindness of the man they called 'Freddie The Great'.

Paul Gambaccini, DJ and rock historian:

"He really gave life and showmanship to the fore. He could hold an audience in the palm of his hand. He and the group absolutely stole Live Aid."

David Bowie:

"We will all miss him a lot.
Together with Queen he made a great contribution to popular music."

Francis Rossi of Status Quo:

"Freddie was one of the elite few who could really set a stadium alight. Along with millions of fans throughout the world, I will miss his exceptional performance and brilliant voice."

George Michael:

"Freddie was a huge source of inspiration to me. I religiously attended Queen shows year after year and waited eagerly for each new album release."

Andrew Lloyd-Webber

revealed that he had been involved in plans for Freddie to play the lead in the film version of his musical Phantom Of The Opera. He said: "The whole of Hollywood was desperate for Freddie to take the part. He would have been brilliant. He was a master of his craft."

Harvey Goldsmith, music promoter:

"Some of the greatest live shows I've ever been involved in were Queen concerts. Freddie was one of the greatest performers Britain has produced."

Simon Bates, Radio One DJ:

"His great contribution was more than superb musicianship, it was putting sheer fun back in the charts. He sang like a bird and sent himself up rotten."

Phil Collins:

"I admired him and I admired his honesty in admitting he had Aids. It is all so sad."

Neil Sedaka:

"If you loved music, you loved Freddie Mercury.
He was a stunning showman who will be truly missed."

Screaming Lord Sutch:

"Like Presley he had the looks, physique, movement and that outrageous voice. It was almost like he had too much talent to pack into one body."

Elton John said in a moving TV tribute:

"Freddie Mercury was an incredible innovative singer and frontman for a band. He was a very good friend of mine and it was a privilege to have known him for some of his life".

"He was very funny, extremely outrageous, very kind and he was a great musician - one of the great frontmen of rock 'n' roll bands. It is very hard to be a frontman. It is not many who have pulled it off. You can think of Jagger, Daltrey and then you can think of Freddie Mercury".

"Freddie always had a sense of humour, a sense of outrage, and he stole the show at Live Aid. Quite simply, he was one of the most important figures in rock 'n' roll in the last 20 years".

"I will miss him - we will all miss him - for his music, his humanity. But the great thing is that we still have his music to remember him by. We will remember that Freddie Mercury was something special."

Brian May, Roger Taylor, John Deacon and Jim Beach (Manager):

"We have lost the greatest and most beloved member of our family. We feel overwhelming grief that he has gone, sadness that he should be cut down at the height of his creativity, but above all pride in the courageous way that he lived and died. As soon as we are able we would like to celebrate his life in the style to which he was accustomed."